Searchlight
BOOKS™

Spy Secrets

Secret

Spy Hacks

Christy Peterson

Lerner Publications ◆ Minneapolis

Lerner Publications Company
An imprint of Lerner Publishing Group, Inc.
241 First Avenue North
Minneapolis, MN 55401 USA

For reading levels and more information, look up this title
at www.lernerbooks.com.

Main body text set in Adrianna Regular.
Typeface provided by Chank.

Editor: Brianna Kaiser **Designer:** Mary Ross **Photo Editor:** Brianna Kaiser

Library of Congress Cataloging-in-Publication Data

Names: Peterson, Christy, author.
Title: Secret Spy Hacks / Christy Peterson.
Description: Minneapolis : Lerner Publications, [2021] | Series: Searchlight books. Spy
    secrets | Includes bibliographical references and index. | Audience: Ages 8–11 |
    Audience: Grades 2–3 | Summary: "Spies have lots of tools and tricks up their
    sleeves that help them do the jobs they do. This book gives the inside scoop on all
    the fascinating tricks of the trade!"— Provided by publisher.
Identifiers: LCCN 2020010372 (print) | LCCN 2020010373 (ebook) |
    ISBN 9781728404271 (library binding) | ISBN 9781728418667 (ebook)
Subjects: LCSH: Intelligence service—Technological innovations—Juvenile literature. |
    Intelligence service—Methodology—Juvenile literature.
Classification: LCC JF1525.I6 P479 2021 (print) | LCC JF1525.I6 (ebook) | DDC 327.12—
    dc23

LC record available at https://lccn.loc.gov/2020010372
LC ebook record available at https://lccn.loc.gov/2020010373

Manufactured in the United States of America
1-48485-48999-8/20/2020

Table of Contents

Chapter 1

AN UNLIKELY HERO

The German army marched across Europe during World War II (1939–1945). They captured many countries and killed people who resisted. A Spanish man named Juan Pujol was determined to help the Allies defeat Germany. In 1941, he offered to spy for the British. But the British didn't trust him. They refused to hire him.

Pujol formed a new plan. He would pretend to spy for the Germans. Then he could offer to be a double agent for the British. Pujol learned everything he could about Germany. He practiced his act. He convinced the Germans that he was a reliable source. They began paying him for information.

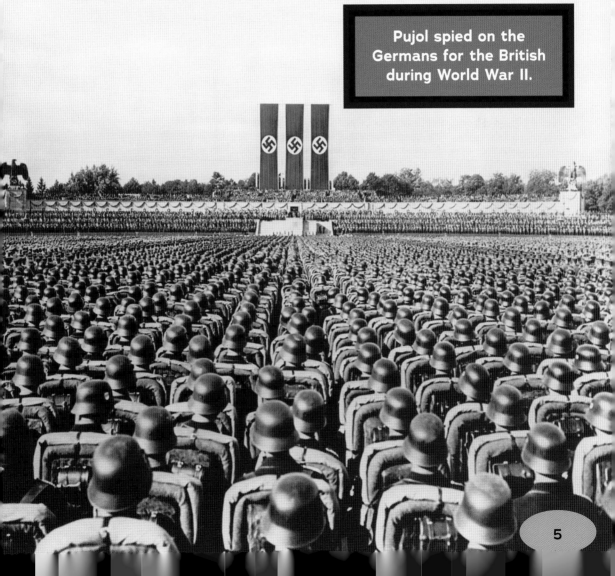

Pujol spied on the Germans for the British during World War II.

In time, Pujol had twenty-seven secret agents working with him to send British secrets to the Germans. But the agents and the secrets were fake. The British noticed the Germans preparing for battles that never happened. This convinced the British that they could trust Pujol. His work helped the British and their allies defeat the Germans.

PUJOL SENT FAKE BRITISH SECRETS TO THE GERMANS.

▼

Spies are always collecting information.

The Best of the Best

Agents such as Pujol were successful because they mastered their tradecraft. Tradecraft is the tricks and tools spies use to do their job well. During wartime, agents help their side defeat an enemy in battle. But spies are equally important during peacetime. They help keep their countries safe by collecting information about their enemies.

Photography is one way spies can obtain secret information.

Spies are experts at many skills. They move sneakily to avoid being discovered. They use covers and tools to obtain secret information. Then they carefully pass along the secret information. Spies train hard to prepare for any situation.

That's a Fact!

In 1942, an unlikely group of spies left the US for Europe. They were librarians. Their job was to collect magazines, newspapers, and books. A newspaper or magazine might seem like an odd place to look for military secrets. But finding useful information doesn't always mean sneaking into hidden locations or listening in on secret conversations. Sometimes a news story might give clues about what an enemy is planning.

Chapter 2

ATTENTION TO DETAIL

A secret agent trains a lot before leaving on a mission. Secret agents in World War II learned to communicate in secret. They also learned to handle weapons and explosives. But their training would have been useless without good covers. If someone revealed a spy's identity, the spy would be captured at once.

Agents learned details about everyday life in their assigned country. They had to learn how to dress and act so they could blend in. They even had to pay attention to how their clothes were made. Incorrect details could give a spy away. Spy agencies bought clothes from other countries. They took the clothes apart so they could copy them exactly.

Spies have to learn details about clothing and everyday life of other countries to blend in.

PEOPLE HOLD FORKS IN DIFFERENT HANDS DEPENDING ON WHERE THEY LIVE.

Attention to detail is essential for a modern spy too. American spies working in European countries learn a few tricks to blend in. They put their weight on both of their legs instead of just one, the way Americans tend to do. They learn to hold their forks in their left hands. They leave their favorite baseball caps at home. Blending in helps a spy complete missions.

Helpful Gadgets

Gadgets also help spies do their jobs. Sometimes these gadgets are hidden inside other objects. But sometimes the smartest trick is to not hide the gadget at all. One American spy agency created a camera with a tiny hole in the lens cover. An agent could take photos when people thought the camera wasn't being used.

A camera with a hole in the lens cover can take photos secretly.

Agencies also create tools to keep agents safe. In the 1970s, spies wore a gadget called an SRR-100. The SRR-100 could pick up radio signals. It came with an earpiece that looked like an actual ear. If agents from another country were nearby, the spy heard their communication. This way a spy knew if they were being followed.

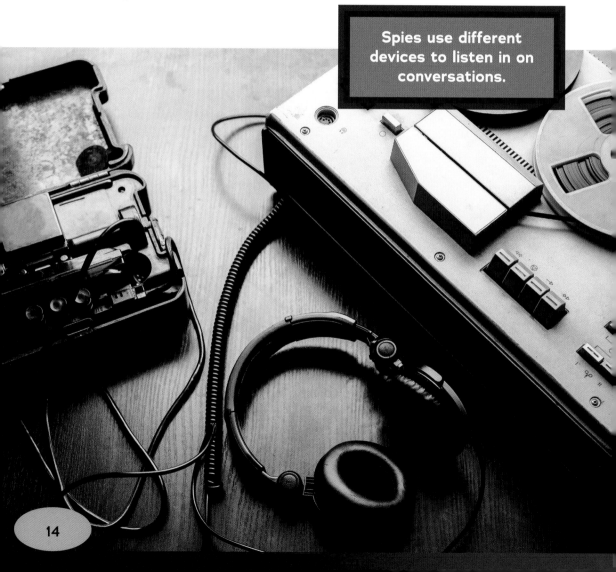

Spies use different devices to listen in on conversations.

EVERYDAY OBJECTS, LIKE EMPTY WALNUT SHELLS, CAN HIDE CODES AND MESSAGES.

Not all tools are high tech. Spies in World War I (1914–1918) wrote in code on the backs of buttons. World War II agents carried small, sharp hooks. They used them to slash the tires of enemy vehicles. Spies from the Soviet Union (a former nation of republics that included Russia) hid codes inside empty walnut shells. A smart spy uses all available tools.

That's a Fact!

In World War I, countries took photos from high in the air to spy on their enemies. But planes in those days flew low and slow. Pilots were in danger of being shot down. So military spies came up with a sneaky way to get the pictures. They attached cameras to pigeons. Pigeons were common, and no one paid attention to them. Spy agencies used these feathered agents well into the twentieth century.

Spy agencies used pigeons to spy on their enemies in World War I.

Chapter 3

HIDDEN COMMUNICATION

Successful spies must be able to think quickly to get out of trouble. During the Civil War (1861–1865), Elizabeth Van Lew visited soldiers who had been captured. She brought them food in a special dish. The food went in the upper part of the dish, and boiling water went in the lower part. This kept the food hot.

Elizabeth Van Lew
was a spy during
the Civil War.

But Van Lew didn't put hot water in the bottom.
She used the space to sneak in supplies and messages.
The guards became suspicious. Van Lew heard that they
planned to inspect the dish. The next time she visited the
prison, she filled the compartment with exactly what was
supposed to go there. The guard who searched the dish
found only hot water.

Passing on Secrets

Spies have tricks for communicating in secret. One clever way to pass information is to hide it in a picture. Computer images are made up of thousands of tiny dots. An agent can replace one of the dots with a message. This message can't be seen unless that particular dot is enlarged many times. Hiding a message inside an image is called steganography.

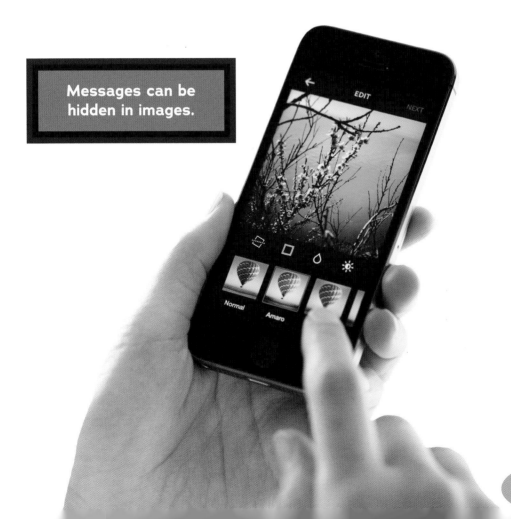

Messages can be hidden in images.

A SPY MAY WRITE A MESSAGE WITH A TYPEWRITER OR INVISIBLE INK INSTEAD OF A COMPUTER.

But sending messages by computer is still risky. Spies on the other side can steal the information and decode it. Sometimes agents rely on older tools to avoid this. They might use a typewriter or invisible ink instead. Since these methods are rarely used, enemy agents may not look for them.

Written communication is not always possible. Agents use whatever they have on hand. Spies during World War II sometimes used clothes hanging on a clothesline to send a message. The secret word was made up of the first letter of each item of clothing. A clothesline with a robe, underwear, and a nightgown would mean "run."

A clothesline can send spies messages.

Meet a Spy!

The Central Intelligence Agency (CIA) had a big problem. Its agents in the Soviet Union kept getting caught. In 1985, the agency put Jeanne Vertefeuille and her team on the case. The team discovered that a certain CIA employee seemed to have much more money than he should. The employee, Aldrich Ames, also made big bank deposits after visits to the Soviet embassy. Thanks to Vertefeuille and her team, Ames was arrested for spying.

Jeanne Vertefeuille (*center*) and her spy team

Chapter 4

A QUICK GETAWAY

A spy moves through a crowd. She is being followed by counterintelligence agents. They are sure to arrest her if she cannot escape. The crowd is preventing her from getting away. She needs a solution—and quickly. She keeps moving.

The spy takes off her suit coat and stuffs it in her bag. She pulls her hair back into a ponytail. She puts on glasses and a floppy hat. Then she grabs headphones and pretends to listen to music. In only a few seconds, she has become someone else. This trick is called a quick change. It leads enemy agents to believe they have lost the person they were tailing.

Spies on the go change their appearance to escape enemy agents.

Meet a Spy!

Harriet Tubman is famous for helping slaves escape. But she was also a spy during the Civil War. She snuck into enemy territory many times to carry out missions. She often disguised herself as a farmworker or a farm wife. Her most famous mission took place in May 1863. She led a raid in South Carolina. She and her team destroyed supplies and rescued more than eight hundred slaves.

Keeping Spies Safe

Spy agencies teach agents other skills to keep them safe. One trick spies learn is called a brush pass. A spy and another person pass on a sidewalk. They don't make eye contact. They hand off an object to each other while they are walking. The goal is to do this quickly and smoothly. Even a person walking right next to them wouldn't notice.

Spies can hand off messages without people around them noticing.

SPY AGENCIES CAN USE PLANES TO RESCUE THEIR SPIES.

Spies work hard to go unnoticed. But sometimes agencies need to make a dramatic rescue. One rescue tool was called Skyhook. To use Skyhook, agents inflated a helium balloon attached to a 500-foot (152 m) cable. They strapped themselves to the cable and let the balloon fly into the air. A plane flew overhead and grabbed the cable. The agents rose into the air, and they were pulled into the plane.

A spy could master the skill of flying a plane or a helicopter to help on missions.

Spies do their work to keep people safe and to give their side an advantage. But spying is dangerous work. To reduce the risk of getting caught, spy agencies give their agents lots of training. Most important, they teach spies to solve problems. A quick-thinking spy who has mastered many tools and tricks is most likely to succeed.

I Spy!

Dead drops are places where agents and their contacts exchange items. You can use a dead drop to trade secret messages with friends. If your dead drop is in the kitchen, you could leave a message in an empty food container in a cupboard. In a closet, you might leave it in the pocket of a coat or inside a shoe. In a garage, you might use an old toolbox. The key is to select an unused object that fits in with its surroundings.

Glossary

Allies: countries that joined together as unified forces in World War I and World War II

brush pass: a brief meeting between an agent and a contact to exchange information

counterintelligence: individuals working to keep enemy spies from gaining secret information

cover: a secret identity

double agent: a spy who pretends to spy for one country but really spies on that country for another country

quick change: changing clothes and accessories quickly to hide one's identity, usually in a crowd

secret agent: a person who steals secret information and passes it along to a spy agency. Secret agents are also called spies.

spy agency: an organization that collects and analyzes secret information

steganography: hiding secret information in images or in audio or video recordings

tradecraft: tricks and tools used in spying

Learn More

Central Intelligence Agency—Spy Kids
https://www.cia.gov/kids-page/

Denson, Bryan. *Catching a Russian Spy: Agent Les G. Wiser Jr. and the Case of Aldrich Ames.* New York: Roaring Brook, 2020.

Ducksters: World War II Spies and Secret Agents
https://www.ducksters.com/history/world_war_ii/spies_and_secret_agents_of_ww2.php

International Spy Museum: "Language of Espionage"
https://www.spymuseum.org/education-programs/spy-resources/language-of-espionage/

Peterson, Christy. *Secret Spy Codes and Messages.* Minneapolis: Lerner Publications, 2021.

Rockwell, Anne. *A Spy Called James: The True Story of James Lafayette, Revolutionary War Double Agent.* Minneapolis: Carolrhoda Books, 2016.

Index

Photo Acknowledgments

Image credits: Everett Collection/Shutterstock.com, p. 5; Steve Scott/Shutterstock.com, p. 6; Gorodenkoff/Shutterstock.com, p. 7; FXQuadro/Shutterstock.com, p. 8; Mitzo/Shutterstock.com, p. 9; Settawat Udom/Shutterstock.com, p. 11; Aleksandr; Lupin/Shutterstock.com, p. 12; Svitlana Kataieva/Shutterstock.com, p. 13; Only_NewPhoto/Shutterstock.com, p. 14; AlenKadr/Shutterstock.com, p. 15; Boyer/Roger Viollet/Getty Images, p. 16; Lebrecht Music & Arts/Alamy Stock Photo, p. 18; Bloomicon/Shutterstock.com, p. 19; Triff/Shutterstock.com, p. 20; PaytonVanGorp/Shutterstock.com, p. 21; United States Central Intelligence Agency, p. 22; goofyfoottaka/Shutterstock.com, p. 24; Abecedare/Wikimedia Commons, p. 25; IDEAPIXEL/Shutterstock.com, p. 26; Mike Focus/Shutterstock.com, p. 27; Dmytro Zinkevych/Shutterstock.com, p. 28.

Cover: Boyer/Roger Viollet/Getty Images.